ALABASTER

ALABASTER

Printed in Canada

Contact
hello@alabasterco.com
www.alabasterco.com

Alabaster Co. The Bible Beautiful.
Visual imagery & thoughtful design integrated within the Bible.
Cultivating conversation between art, beauty, & faith.

Founded in 2016.

NLT.

ARTIST INTRODUCTION

———

At its crux, the Book of Ecclesiastes highlights the absurdities of life. Guided by the words of "The Teacher" (Eccl 1:1), the book begins with "Everything is meaningless, completely meaningless!" The word translated as meaningless is the Hebrew word, *hevel*. It literally translates into "vapor" or "breath"— which, in the context of the book, indicates the idea of something "fleeting."

Ecclesiastes is simultaneously a book about life and death. Extending beyond an emotional experience, death is posed as an inevitable part of life—they are two sides of the same coin. The book reflects on death and how it should inform our time in life. It is a book that explores both optimism and pessimism within the human experience.

In making this book, we reflect on these themes by opening with ephemeral images and faint elements— image movements and transparencies to encapsulate the spirit of *hevel*. We continue with wispy landscapes, natural elements, and temporary materials, all to explore the diverse *hevel* world we journey through as human beings.

Ultimately, Ecclesiastes shows us that everything is fleeting and much of life is beyond our control. And yet, there are quiet invitations beneath the surface: to do our best in everything, to be wise, and to find enjoyment in the small things. Even as *hevel* is part of the natural human experience, may we choose to embrace contentment in the present, release anxious worries about the future, and trust in God. Amen.

BOOK OF

ECCLESIASTES

1

¹ These are the words of the Teacher, King David's son, who ruled in Jerusalem.

EVERYTHING IS MEANINGLESS

² "Everything is meaningless," says the Teacher, "completely meaningless!" ³ What do people get for all their hard work under the sun? ⁴ Generations come and generations go, but the earth never changes. ⁵ The sun rises and the sun sets, then hurries around to rise again. ⁶ The wind blows south, and then turns north. Around and around it goes, blowing in circles. ⁷ Rivers run into the sea, but the sea is never full. Then the water returns again to the rivers and flows out again to the sea. ⁸ Everything is wearisome beyond description. No matter how much we see, we are never satisfied. No matter how much we hear, we are not content.

[9] History merely repeats itself. It has all been done before. Nothing under the sun is truly new. [10] Sometimes people say, "Here is something new!" But actually it is old; nothing is ever truly new. [11] We don't remember what happened in the past, and in future generations, no one will remember what we are doing now.

THE TEACHER SPEAKS: THE FUTILITY OF WISDOM

[12] I, the Teacher, was king of Israel, and I lived in Jerusalem. [13] I devoted myself to search for understanding and to explore by wisdom everything being done under heaven. I soon discovered that God has dealt a tragic existence to the human race. [14] I observed everything going on under the sun, and really, it is all meaningless—like chasing the wind. [15] What is wrong cannot be made right. What is missing cannot be recovered. [16] I said to myself, "Look, I am wiser than any of the kings who ruled in Jerusalem before me. I have greater wisdom and knowledge than any of them." [17] So I set out to learn everything from wisdom to madness and folly. But I learned firsthand that pursuing all this is like chasing the wind. [18] The greater my wisdom, the greater my grief. To increase knowledge only increases sorrow.

2

THE FUTILITY OF PLEASURE

[1] I said to myself, "Come on, let's try pleasure. Let's look for the 'good things' in life." But I found that this, too, was meaningless. [2] So I said, "Laughter is silly. What good does it do to seek pleasure?" [3] After much thought, I decided to cheer myself with wine. And while still seeking wisdom, I clutched at foolishness. In this way, I tried to experience the only happiness most people find during their brief life in this world.

[4] I also tried to find meaning by building huge homes for myself and by planting beautiful vineyards. [5] I made gardens and parks, filling them with all kinds of fruit trees. [6] I built reservoirs to collect the water to irrigate my many flourishing groves. [7] I bought slaves, both men and women, and others were born into my household. I also owned large herds and flocks, more than any of the kings who had lived in Jerusalem before me. [8] I collected great sums of silver and gold, the treasure of many kings and provinces. I hired wonderful singers, both men and women, and had many beautiful concubines. I had everything a man could desire! [9] So I became greater than all who had lived in Jerusalem before me, and my wisdom never failed me. [10] Anything I wanted, I would take. I denied myself no pleasure. I even found great pleasure in hard work, a reward for all my labors. [11] But as I looked at everything I had worked so hard to accomplish, it was all so meaningless—like chasing the wind. There was nothing really worthwhile anywhere.

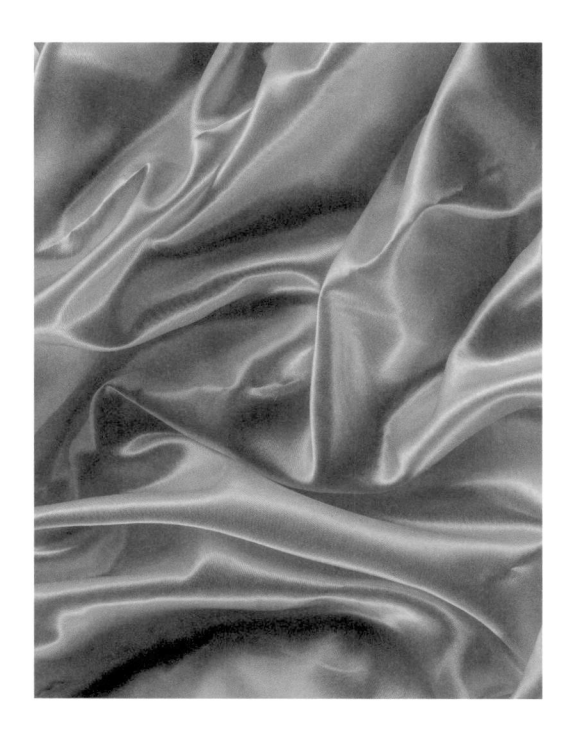

THE WISE AND THE FOOLISH

[12] So I decided to compare wisdom with foolishness and madness (for who can do this better than I, the king?). [13] I thought, "Wisdom is better than foolishness, just as light is better than darkness. [14] For the wise can see where they are going, but fools walk in the dark." Yet I saw that the wise and the foolish share the same fate. [15] Both will die. So I said to myself, "Since I will

end up the same as the fool, what's the value of all my wisdom? This is all so meaningless!" [16] For the wise and the foolish both die. The wise will not be remembered any longer than the fool. In the days to come, both will be forgotten. [17] So I came to hate life because everything done here under the sun is so troubling. Everything is meaningless—like chasing the wind.

THE FUTILITY OF WORK

[18] I came to hate all my hard work here on earth, for I must leave to others everything I have earned. [19] And who can tell whether my successors will be wise or foolish? Yet they will control everything I have gained by my skill and hard work under the sun. How meaningless! [20] So I gave up in despair, questioning the value of all my hard work in this world. [21] Some people work wisely with knowledge and skill, then must leave the fruit of their efforts to someone who hasn't worked for it. This, too, is meaningless, a great tragedy. [22] So what do people get in this life for all their hard work and anxiety? [23] Their days of labor are filled with pain and grief; even at night their minds cannot rest. It is all meaningless. [24] So I decided there is nothing better than to enjoy food and drink and to find satisfaction in work. Then I realized that these pleasures are from the hand of God. [25] For who can eat or enjoy anything apart from him? [26] God gives wisdom, knowledge, and joy to those who please him. But if a sinner becomes wealthy, God takes the wealth away and gives it to those who please him. This, too, is meaningless—like chasing the wind.

3

A TIME FOR EVERYTHING

1 For everything there is a season,
   a time for every activity under heaven.
2 A time to be born and a time to die.
   A time to plant and a time to harvest.

[3] A time to kill and a time to heal.

A time to tear down and a time to build up.

[4] A time to cry and a time to laugh.

A time to grieve and a time to dance.

[5] A time to scatter stones and a time to gather stones.

A time to embrace and a time to turn away.

[6] A time to search and a time to quit searching.

A time to keep and a time to throw away.

[7] A time to tear and a time to mend.

A time to be quiet and a time to speak.

[8] A time to love and a time to hate.

A time for war and a time for peace.

[9] What do people really get for all their hard work? [10] I have seen the burden God has placed on us all. [11] Yet God has made everything beautiful for its own time. He has planted eternity in the human heart, but even so, people cannot see the whole scope of God's work from beginning to end. [12] So I concluded there is nothing better than to be happy and enjoy ourselves as long as we can. [13] And people should eat and drink and enjoy the fruits of their labor, for these are gifts from God. [14] And I know that whatever God does is final. Nothing can be added to it or taken from it. God's purpose is that people should fear him. [15] What is happening now has happened before, and what will happen in the future has happened before, because God makes the same things happen over and over again.

THE INJUSTICES OF LIFE

[16] I also noticed that under the sun there is evil in the courtroom. Yes, even the courts of law are corrupt! [17] I said to myself, "In due season God will judge everyone, both good and bad, for all their deeds." [18] I also thought about the human condition—how God proves to people that they are like animals. [19] For people and animals share the same fate—both breathe and both must die. So people have no real advantage over the animals. How meaningless! [20] Both go to the same place—they came from dust and they return to dust. [21] For who can prove that the human spirit goes up and the spirit of animals goes down into the earth? [22] So I saw that there is nothing better for people than to be happy in their work. That is our lot in life. And no one can bring us back to see what happens after we die.

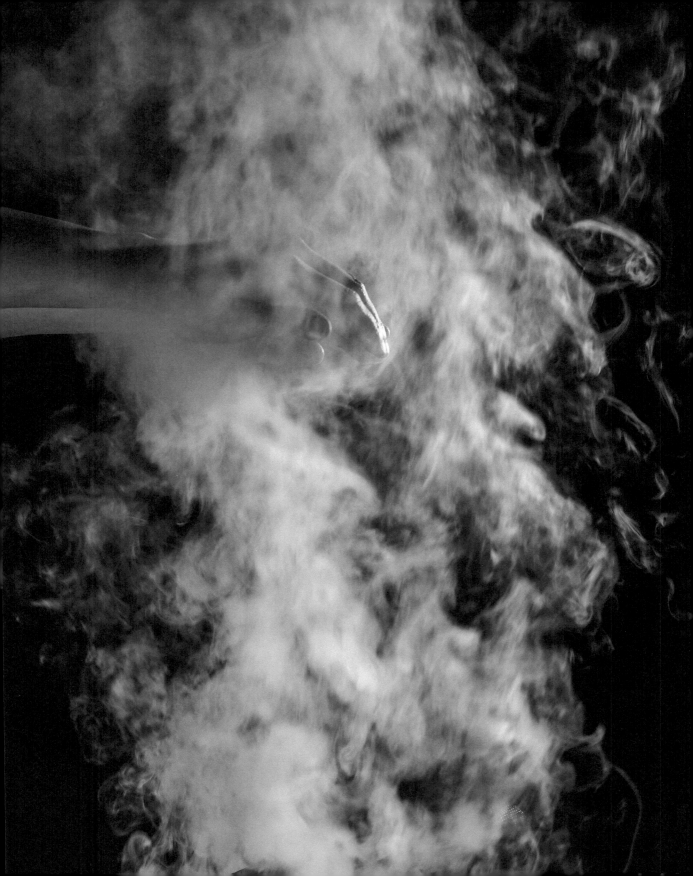

4

[1] Again, I observed all the oppression that takes place under the sun. I saw the tears of the oppressed, with no one to comfort them. The oppressors have great power, and their victims are helpless. [2] So I concluded that the dead are better off than the living. [3] But most fortunate of all are those who are not yet born. For they have not seen all the evil that is done under the sun. [4] Then I observed that most people are motivated to success because they envy their neighbors. But this, too, is meaningless—like chasing the wind. [5] "Fools fold their idle hands, leading them to ruin." [6] And yet, "Better to have one handful with quietness than two handfuls with hard work and chasing the wind."

THE ADVANTAGES OF COMPANIONSHIP

[7] I observed yet another example of something meaningless under the sun. [8] This is the case of a man who is all alone, without a child or a brother, yet who works hard to gain as much wealth as he can. But then he asks himself, "Who am I working for? Why am I giving up so much pleasure now?" It is all so meaningless and depressing. [9] Two people are better off than one, for they can help each other succeed. [10] If one person falls, the other can reach out and help. But someone who falls alone is in real trouble. [11] Likewise, two people lying close together can keep each other warm. But how can one be warm alone? [12] A person standing alone can be attacked and defeated, but two can stand back-to-back and conquer. Three are even better, for a triple-braided cord is not easily broken.

THE FUTILITY OF POLITICAL POWER

[13] It is better to be a poor but wise youth than an old and foolish king who refuses all advice. [14] Such a youth could rise from poverty and succeed. He might even become king, though he has been in prison. [15] But then everyone rushes to the side of yet another youth who replaces him. [16] Endless crowds stand around him, but then another generation grows up and rejects him, too. So it is all meaningless—like chasing the wind.

5

APPROACHING GOD WITH CARE

[1] As you enter the house of God, keep your ears open and your mouth shut. It is evil to make mindless offerings to God. [2] Don't make rash promises, and don't be hasty in bringing matters before God. After all, God is in heaven, and you are here on earth. So let your words be few.

[3] Too much activity gives you restless dreams; too many words make you a fool.

[4] When you make a promise to God, don't delay in following through, for God takes no pleasure in fools. Keep all the promises you make to him. [5] It is better to say nothing than to make a promise and not keep it. [6] Don't let your mouth make you sin. And don't defend yourself by telling the Temple messenger that the promise you made was a mistake. That would make God angry, and he might wipe out everything you have achieved. [7] Talk is cheap, like daydreams and other useless activities. Fear God instead.

THE FUTILITY OF WEALTH

[8] Don't be surprised if you see a poor person being oppressed by the powerful and if justice is being miscarried throughout the land. For every official is under orders from higher up, and matters of justice get lost in red tape and bureaucracy. [9] Even the king milks the land for his own profit! [10] Those who love

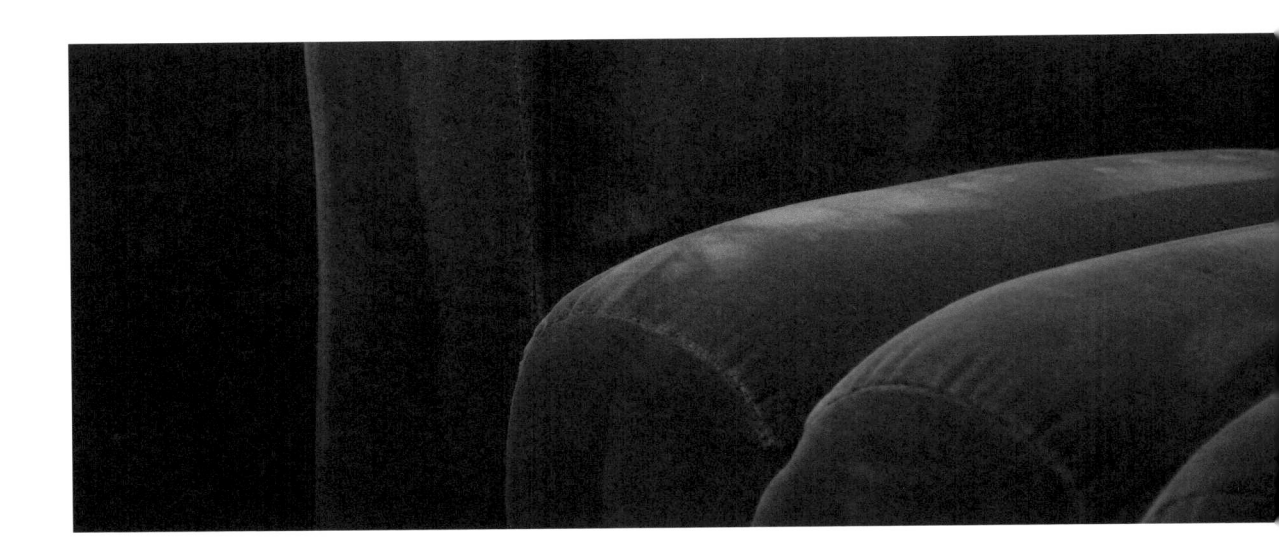

money will never have enough. How meaningless to think that wealth brings true happiness! [11] The more you have, the more people come to help you spend it. So what good is wealth—except perhaps to watch it slip through your fingers! [12] People who work hard sleep well, whether they eat little or much. But the rich seldom get a good night's sleep. [13] There is another serious problem I have seen under the sun. Hoarding riches harms the saver. [14] Money is put into risky investments that turn sour, and everything is lost. In the end, there is nothing left to pass on to one's children. [15] We all come to the end of our lives as naked and empty-handed as on the day we were born. We can't take our riches with us.

[16] And this, too, is a very serious problem. People leave this world no better off than when they came. All their hard work is for nothing—like working for the wind. [17] Throughout their lives, they live under a cloud—frustrated, discouraged, and angry.

[18] Even so, I have noticed one thing, at least, that is good. It is good for people to eat, drink, and enjoy their work under the sun during the short life God has given them, and to accept their lot in life. [19] And it is a good thing to receive wealth from God and the good health to enjoy it. To enjoy your work and accept your lot in life—this is indeed a gift from God. [20] God keeps such people so busy enjoying life that they take no time to brood over the past.

6

¹ There is another serious tragedy I have seen under the sun, and it weighs heavily on humanity. ² God gives some people great wealth and honor and everything they could ever want, but then he doesn't give them the chance to enjoy these things. They die, and someone else, even a stranger, ends up enjoying their wealth! This is meaningless—a sickening tragedy. ³ A man might have a hundred children and live to be very old. But if he finds no satisfaction in life and doesn't even get a decent burial, it would have been better for him to be born dead. ⁴ His birth would have been meaningless, and he would have ended in darkness. He wouldn't even have had a name, ⁵ and he would never have seen the sun or known of its existence. Yet he would have had more peace than in growing up to be an unhappy man. ⁶ He might live a thousand years twice over but still not find contentment. And since he must die like everyone else—well, what's the use?

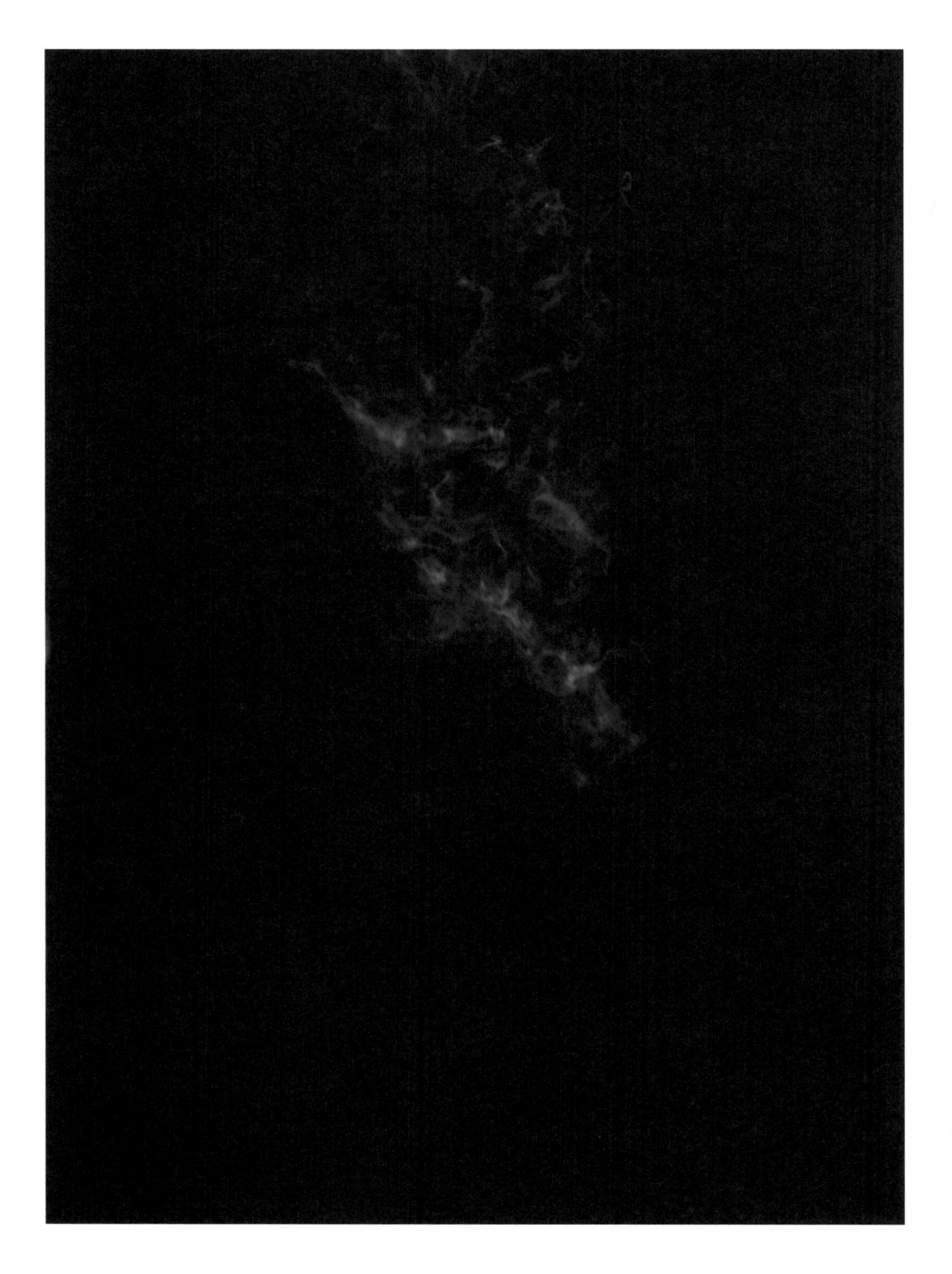

[7] All people spend their lives scratching for food, but they never seem to have enough. [8] So are wise people really better off than fools? Do poor people gain anything by being wise and knowing how to act in front of others?

CHAPTER 6

[9] Enjoy what you have rather than desiring what you don't have. Just dreaming about nice things is meaningless—like chasing the wind.

THE FUTURE—DETERMINED AND UNKNOWN

[10] Everything has already been decided. It was known long ago what each person would be. So there's no use arguing with God about your destiny. [11] The more words you speak, the less they mean. So what

good are they? [12] In the few days of our meaningless lives, who knows how our days can best be spent? Our lives are like a shadow. Who can tell what will happen on this earth after we are gone?

7

WISDOM FOR LIFE

1 A good reputation is more valuable than costly perfume.
And the day you die is better than the day you are born.
2 Better to spend your time at funerals than at parties.
After all, everyone dies—
so the living should take this to heart.

[3] Sorrow is better than laughter,
for sadness has a refining influence on us.
[4] A wise person thinks a lot about death,
while a fool thinks only about having a good time.

⁵ Better to be criticized by a wise person
than to be praised by a fool.

⁶ A fool's laughter is quickly gone,
like thorns crackling in a fire.
This also is meaningless.

7 Extortion turns wise people into fools,
and bribes corrupt the heart.

8 Finishing is better than starting.
Patience is better than pride.

9 Control your temper,
for anger labels you a fool.

10 Don't long for "the good old days."
This is not wise.

11 Wisdom is even better when you have money.
Both are a benefit as you go through life.

12 Wisdom and money can get you almost anything,
but only wisdom can save your life.

13 Accept the way God does things,
for who can straighten what he has made crooked?

14 Enjoy prosperity while you can,
but when hard times strike, realize that
both come from God.
Remember that nothing is certain in this life.

THE LIMITS OF HUMAN WISDOM

[15] I have seen everything in this meaningless life, including the death of good young people and the long life of wicked people. [16] So don't be too good or too wise! Why destroy yourself? [17] On the other hand, don't be too wicked either. Don't be a fool! Why die before your time? [18] Pay attention to these instructions, for anyone who fears God will avoid both extremes. [19] One wise person is stronger than ten leading citizens of a town! [20] Not a single person on earth is always good and never sins. [21] Don't eavesdrop on others—you may hear your servant curse you. [22] For you know how often you yourself have cursed others. [23] I have always tried my best to let wisdom guide my thoughts and actions. I said to myself, "I am determined to be wise." But it didn't work. [24] Wisdom is always distant and difficult to find. [25] I searched everywhere, determined to find wisdom and to understand the reason for things. I was determined to prove to myself that wickedness is stupid and that foolishness is madness.

[26] I discovered that a seductive woman is a trap more bitter than death. Her passion is a snare, and her soft hands are chains. Those who are pleasing to God will escape her, but sinners will be caught in her snare. [27] "This is my conclusion," says the Teacher. "I discovered this after looking at the matter from every possible angle. [28] Though I have searched repeatedly, I have not found what I was looking for. Only one out of a thousand men is virtuous, but not one woman! [29] But I did find this: God created people to be virtuous, but they have each turned to follow their own downward path."

8

[1] How wonderful to be wise,
    to analyze and interpret things.
    Wisdom lights up a person's face,
    softening its harshness.

OBEDIENCE TO THE KING

[2] Obey the king since you vowed to God that you would. [3] Don't try to avoid doing your duty, and don't stand with those who plot evil, for the king can do whatever he wants. [4] His command is backed by great power. No one can resist or question it. [5] Those who obey him will not be punished. Those who are wise will find a time and a way to do what is right, [6] for there is a time and a way for everything, even when a person is in trouble. [7] Indeed, how can people avoid what they don't know is going to happen? [8] None of us can hold back our spirit from departing. None of us has the power to prevent the day of our death. There is no escaping that obligation, that dark battle. And in the face of death, wickedness will certainly not rescue the wicked.

THE WICKED AND THE RIGHTEOUS

9 I have thought deeply about all that goes on here under the sun, where people have the power to hurt each other. 10 I have seen wicked people buried with honor. Yet they were the very ones who frequented the Temple and are now praised in the same city where they committed their crimes! This, too, is meaningless.

11 When a crime is not punished quickly, people feel it is safe to do wrong. 12 But even though a person sins a hundred times and still lives a long time, I know that those who fear God will be better off. 13 The wicked will not prosper, for they do not fear God. Their days will never grow long like the evening shadows.

[14] And this is not all that is meaningless in our world. In this life, good people are often treated as though they were wicked, and wicked people are often treated as though they were good. This is so meaningless! [15] So I recommend having fun, because there is nothing better for people in this world than to eat, drink, and enjoy life. That way they will experience some happiness along with all the hard work God gives them under the sun. [16] In my search for wisdom and in my observation of people's burdens here on earth, I discovered that there is ceaseless activity, day and night. [17] I realized that no one can discover everything God is doing under the sun. Not even the wisest people discover everything, no matter what they claim.

9

DEATH COMES TO ALL

[1] This, too, I carefully explored: Even though the actions of godly and wise people are in God's hands, no one knows whether God will show them favor. [2] The same destiny ultimately awaits everyone, whether righteous or wicked, good or bad, ceremonially clean or unclean, religious or irreligious. Good people receive the same treatment as sinners, and people who make promises to God are treated like people who don't. [3] It seems so wrong that everyone under the sun suffers the same fate. Already twisted by evil, people choose their own mad course, for they have no hope. There is nothing ahead but death anyway. [4] There is hope only for the living. As they say, "It's better to be a live dog than a dead lion!" [5] The living at least know they will die, but the dead know nothing. They have no further reward, nor are they remembered. [6] Whatever they did in their lifetime— loving, hating, envying—is all long gone. They no longer play a part in anything here on earth. [7] So go ahead. Eat your food with joy, and drink your wine with a happy heart, for God approves of this! [8] Wear fine clothes, with a splash of cologne! [9] Live happily with the woman you love through all the meaningless days of life that God has given you under the sun. The wife God gives you is your reward for all your earthly toil. [10] Whatever you do, do well. For when you go to the grave, there will be no work or planning or knowledge or wisdom.

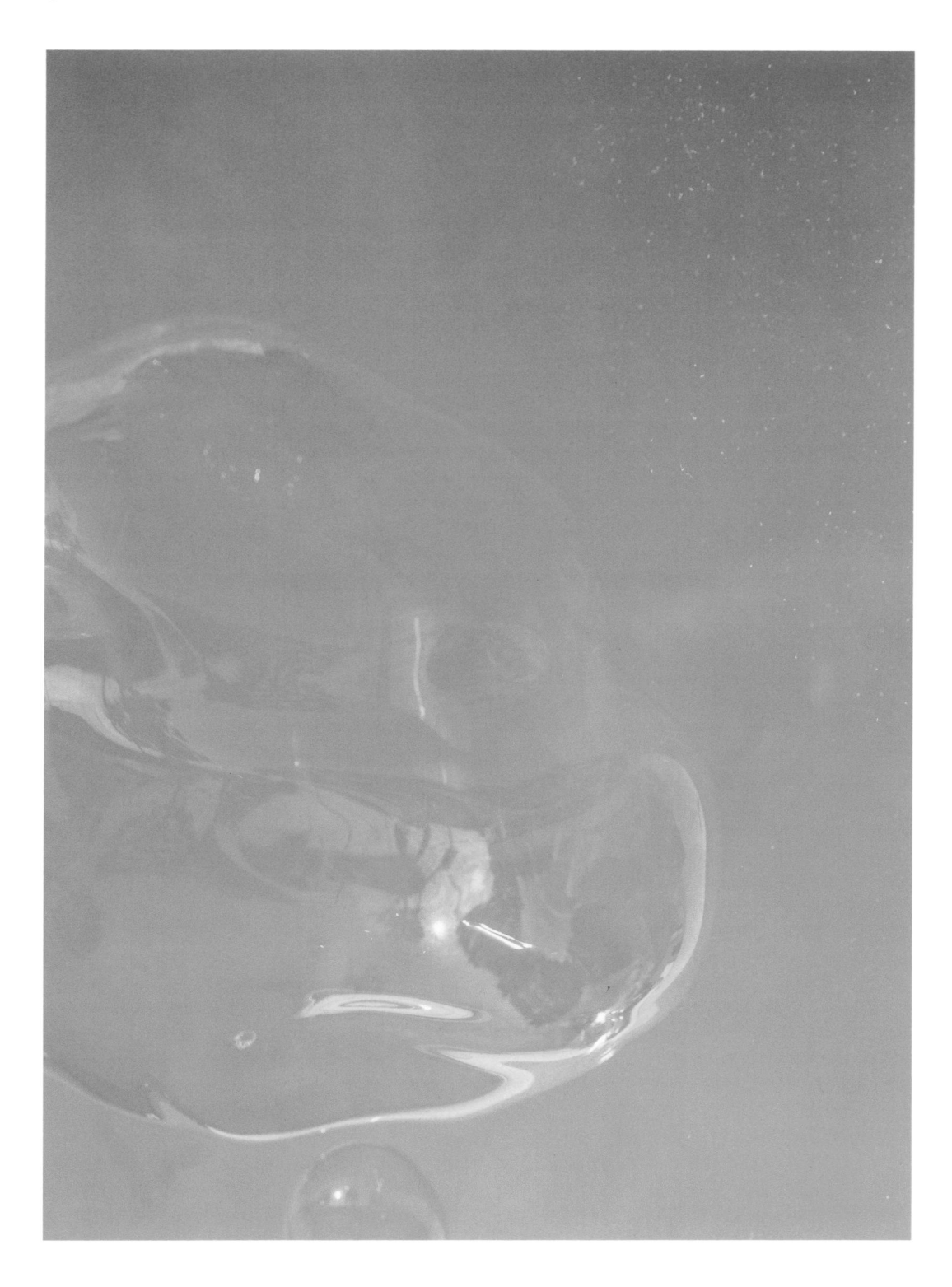

[11] I have observed something else under the sun. The fastest runner doesn't always win the race, and the strongest warrior doesn't always win the battle. The wise sometimes go hungry, and the skillful are not necessarily wealthy. And those who are educated don't always lead successful lives. It is all decided by chance, by being in the right place at the right time. [12] People can never predict when hard times might come. Like fish in a net or birds in a trap, people are caught by sudden tragedy.

THOUGHTS ON WISDOM AND FOLLY

[13] Here is another bit of wisdom that has impressed me as I have watched the way our world works. [14] There was a small town with only a few people, and a great king came with his army and besieged it. [15] A poor, wise man knew how to save the town, and so it was rescued. But afterward no one thought to thank him. [16] So even though wisdom is better than strength, those who are wise will be despised if they are poor. What they say will not be appreciated for long.

[17] Better to hear the quiet words of a wise person
     than the shouts of a foolish king.
[18] Better to have wisdom than weapons of war,
     but one sinner can destroy much that is good.

10

1 As dead flies cause even a bottle of perfume to stink,
so a little foolishness spoils great wisdom and honor.

2 A wise person chooses the right road;
a fool takes the wrong one.

3 You can identify fools
just by the way they walk down the street!

4 If your boss is angry at you, don't quit!
A quiet spirit can overcome even great mistakes.

THE IRONIES OF LIFE

[5] There is another evil I have seen under the sun. Kings and rulers make a grave mistake [6] when they give great authority to foolish people and low positions to people of proven worth. [7] I have even seen servants riding horseback like princes—and princes walking like servants!

[8] When you dig a well,
   you might fall in.
   When you demolish an old wall,
   you could be bitten by a snake.
[9] When you work in a quarry,
   stones might fall and crush you.
   When you chop wood,
   there is danger with each stroke of your ax.

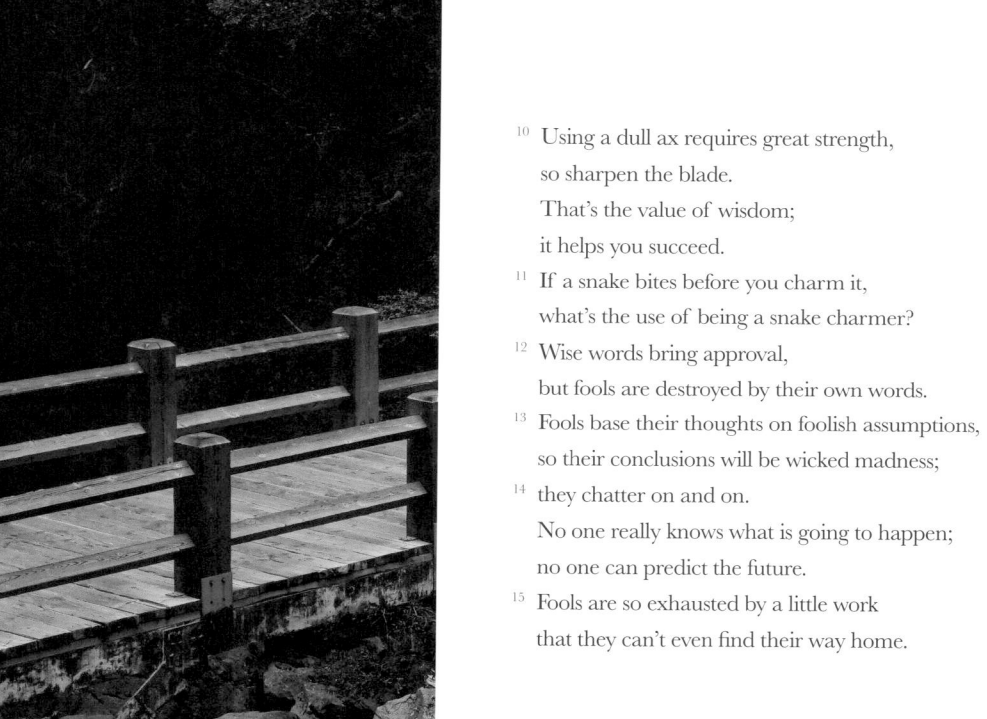

¹⁰ Using a dull ax requires great strength,
   so sharpen the blade.
   That's the value of wisdom;
   it helps you succeed.
¹¹ If a snake bites before you charm it,
   what's the use of being a snake charmer?
¹² Wise words bring approval,
   but fools are destroyed by their own words.
¹³ Fools base their thoughts on foolish assumptions,
   so their conclusions will be wicked madness;
¹⁴ they chatter on and on.
   No one really knows what is going to happen;
   no one can predict the future.
¹⁵ Fools are so exhausted by a little work
   that they can't even find their way home.

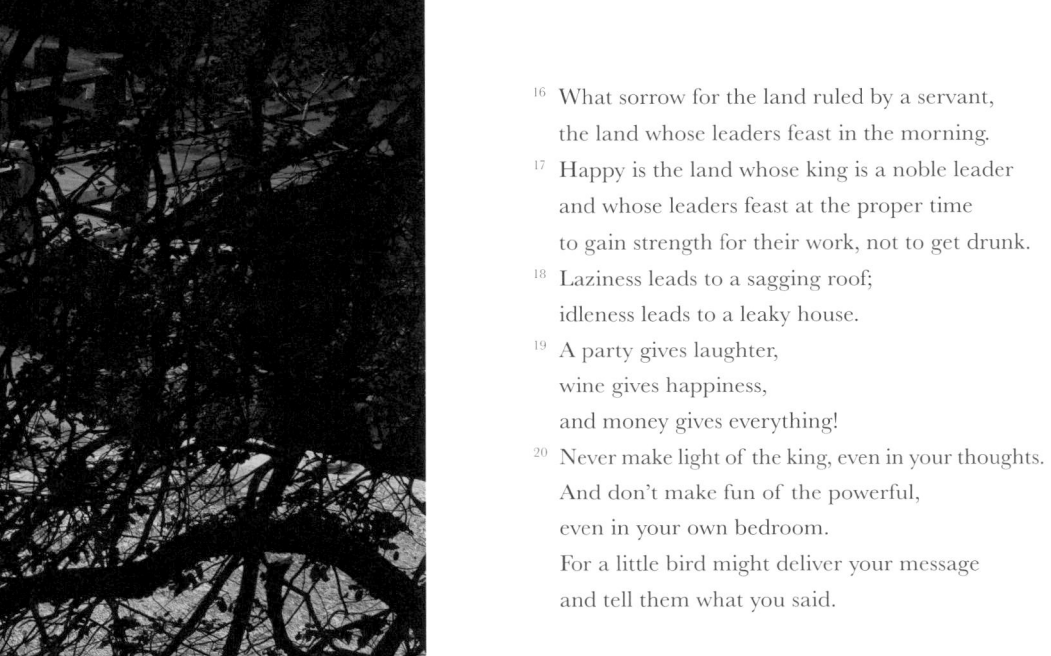

¹⁶ What sorrow for the land ruled by a servant,
the land whose leaders feast in the morning.

¹⁷ Happy is the land whose king is a noble leader
and whose leaders feast at the proper time
to gain strength for their work, not to get drunk.

¹⁸ Laziness leads to a sagging roof;
idleness leads to a leaky house.

¹⁹ A party gives laughter,
wine gives happiness,
and money gives everything!

²⁰ Never make light of the king, even in your thoughts.
And don't make fun of the powerful,
even in your own bedroom.
For a little bird might deliver your message
and tell them what you said.

11

THE UNCERTAINTIES OF LIFE

¹ Send your grain across the seas,
and in time, profits will flow back to you.
² But divide your investments among many places,
for you do not know what risks might lie ahead.
³ When clouds are heavy, the rains come down.
Whether a tree falls north or south, it stays where it falls.
⁴ Farmers who wait for perfect weather never plant.
If they watch every cloud, they never harvest.

[5] Just as you cannot understand the path of the wind or the mystery of a tiny baby growing in its mother's womb, so you cannot understand the activity of God, who does all things. [6] Plant your seed in the morning and keep busy all afternoon, for you don't know if profit will come from one activity or another—or maybe both.

ADVICE FOR YOUNG AND OLD

[7] Light is sweet; how pleasant to see a new day dawning. [8] When people live to be very old, let them rejoice in every day of life. But let them also remember there will be many dark days. Everything still to come is meaningless. [9] Young people, it's wonderful to be young! Enjoy every minute of it. Do everything you want to do; take it all in. But remember that you must give an account to God for everything you do. [10] So refuse to worry, and keep your body healthy. But remember that youth, with a whole life before you, is meaningless.

12

[1] Don't let the excitement of youth cause you to forget your Creator. Honor him in your youth before you grow old and say, "Life is not pleasant anymore." [2] Remember him before the light of the sun, moon, and stars is dim to your old eyes, and rain clouds continually darken your sky. [3] Remember him before your legs—the guards of your house—start to tremble; and before your shoulders—the strong men—stoop. Remember him before your teeth—your few remaining servants—stop grinding; and before your eyes—the women looking through the windows—see dimly. [4] Remember him before the door to life's opportunities is closed and the sound of work fades. Now you rise at the first chirping of the birds, but then all their sounds will grow faint. [5] Remember him before you become fearful of falling and worry about danger in the streets; before your hair turns white like an almond tree in bloom, and you drag along without energy like a dying grasshopper, and the caperberry no longer inspires sexual desire. Remember him before you near the grave, your everlasting home, when the mourners will weep at your funeral. [6] Yes, remember your Creator now while you are young, before the silver cord of life snaps and the golden bowl is broken. Don't wait until the water jar is smashed at the spring and the pulley is broken at the well. [7] For then the dust will return to the earth, and the spirit will return to God who gave it.

CONCLUDING THOUGHTS ABOUT THE TEACHER

[8] "Everything is meaningless," says the Teacher, "completely meaningless." [9] Keep this in mind: The Teacher was considered wise, and he taught the people everything he knew. He listened carefully to many proverbs, studying and classifying them. [10] The Teacher sought to find just the right words to express truths clearly.

[11] The words of the wise are like cattle prods—painful but helpful. Their collected sayings are like a nail-studded stick with which a shepherd drives the sheep. [12] But, my child, let me give you some further advice: Be careful, for writing books is endless, and much study wears you out. [13] That's the whole story. Here now is my final conclusion: Fear God and obey his commands, for this is everyone's duty. [14] God will judge us for everything we do, including every secret thing, whether good or bad.

ALABASTER

BRYAN YE-CHUNG
Co-Founder, Creative Director

BRIAN CHUNG
Co-Founder, Managing Director

WILLA JIN
Operations Director

TYLER ZAK
Product Manager

EMALY HUNTER
Customer Experience Specialist

SAMUEL HAN
Studio Photographer, Cover Image

MINZI BAE
Studio Stylist

JANNA CHRISTIAN
Studio Assistant

DARIN MCKENNA
Content Editor

MATTHEW RAVENELLE
Layout Designer

JOSEPHINE LAW
Original Designer